Quick Revision

KS3

Geography

Laurence Kimpton and David Jones

First published 2007
exclusively for WHSmith by
Hodder Murray, a member of the Hodder Headline group
338 Euston Road
London
NW1 3BH

Impression number   10 9 8 7 6 5 4 3 2 1
Year   2010 2009 2008 2007

A CIP record for this book is available from the British Library.

The right of Laurence Kimpton and David Jones to be identified as the authors of this work has been asserted by them.

Cover illustration by Sally Newton Illustrations.

Typeset by Starfish Design Editorial and Project Management Ltd.

ISBN: 978 0 340 94310 6

Printed and bound in the UK by Hobbs the Printers Ltd.

Climate and weather

Weather is what happens in the atmosphere at a particular time; so we talk about today's weather. **Climate** is the average pattern of weather that we experience over many years. The main elements of weather are temperature, precipitation (rain, snow, hail), air pressure, wind speed and direction, visibility, cloud cover and type, air humidity and sunshine hours.

Climate graphs

Climate graphs show the main features of a place's climate. Mean (average) monthly temperatures are plotted on a line graph and mean monthly rainfall totals on a bar graph. To describe a place's climate from a climate graph you should consider:
- the maximum mean monthly temperature and when it occurs
- the minimum mean monthly temperature and when it occurs
- the annual range of temperature (the difference between the minimum and the maximum)
- the mean annual rainfall total
- how rainfall is distributed over the year.

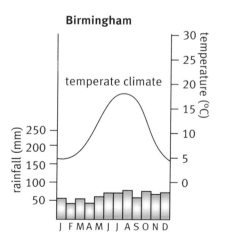

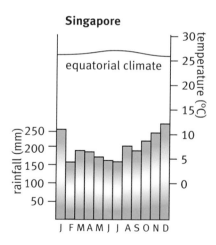

Climatic differences

Temperatures vary from place to place due to several factors:

- **Distance from the Equator** In general, temperatures decrease from the Equator, where the Sun is lower in the sky and so heating is less intense.

- **Land and sea** The sea absorbs heat slowly in summer and releases it slowly in winter. Land heats up quickly in summer and cools quickly in winter. The result is that places near the sea are warmer in winter and cooler in summer than places inland.

- **Ocean currents** Warm ocean currents bring warm water from the tropics to higher latitudes. The warm water increases the temperature of the air above, bringing much warmer conditions in winter than would otherwise be expected. In this way the North Atlantic Drift makes the winter temperatures of western Europe warmer. Cold ocean currents bring cooler temperatures.

- **Altitude** Temperature decreases with increasing height above sea level.

Rainfall totals vary from place to place due to three main factors:

- **Prevailing wind** If the most common wind direction (prevailing wind) is onshore, then a land mass will receive much moisture-laden air from over the ocean. In this way the western coasts of Europe are affected by the prevailing, rain-bearing, south-westerly winds.

- **Distance from the sea** Areas further inland from the sea will be less affected by moisture-laden air from over the oceans.

- **Relief** Mountain areas, especially when close to the sea, will receive much rainfall.

All the factors influencing temperature and rainfall patterns combine with the annual pattern of seasons to give rise to the world's different climatic regions.

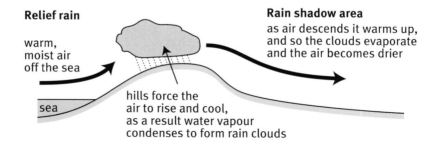

Relief rain

warm, moist air off the sea

sea

hills force the air to rise and cool, as a result water vapour condenses to form rain clouds

Rain shadow area
as air descends it warms up, and so the clouds evaporate and the air becomes drier

Coasts

A coastline of alternating resistant and weak rocks results in **bays and headlands**. Erosion by waves of relatively high ground produces a **cliffed coastline**. Waves erode by water compressing into rocks (**hydraulic action**), by hurling rocks against the bases of cliffs (**corrasion**), by chemical action from the sea water (**corrosion**),

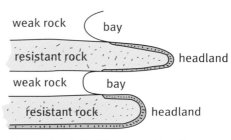

rock fragments grinding each other deep in the water (**attrition**), and by the weight of the waves (**pounding**).

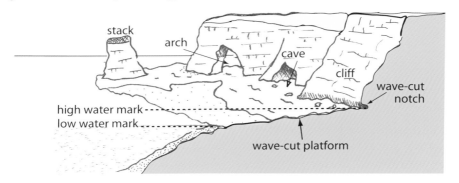

Low-lying coastlines are shaped by waves moving sand and shingle along the coast by **longshore drift**, to form landforms such as **spits** and **bars**.

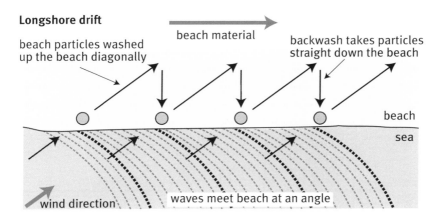

Longshore drift

beach particles washed up the beach diagonally

beach material

backwash takes particles straight down the beach

beach

sea

wind direction

waves meet beach at an angle

Continued overleaf

Spits and bars

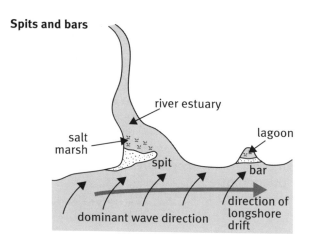

Densely populated areas

The world's people are very unevenly distributed. You can see this from the table which shows how many live in each continent. Within the continents the main densely populated areas are: south and east Asia, Western Europe, the north-eastern USA, the lower Nile valley in Egypt, West Africa and the coastal regions of South America. So we see that only small areas of each continent are densely populated. These densely populated areas actually have over 70% of the world's people.

Within countries, too, population is unevenly distributed, with most people living in particular regions. In the United Kingdom, the most crowded area is the south-east of England, the region which has London at its centre.

Population distribution by continent

continent	population (millions)
Africa	924
Asia	3968
Europe	732
Oceania	34
North America	332
Latin America	566

SEE ALSO Less developed countries (LEDCs), More developed countries (MEDCs), Sparsely populated areas

Deserts

Deserts are the Earth's driest regions. Most deserts are hot deserts with high temperatures throughout the year. Under clear skies, cool nights contrast with hot days. There are three main types of desert landscapes: rugged areas of bare rock, stony plains and sandy deserts. In sandy deserts, wind blows the sand into dunes.

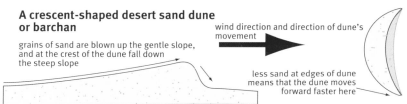

A crescent-shaped desert sand dune or barchan

grains of sand are blown up the gentle slope, and at the crest of the dune fall down the steep slope

wind direction and direction of dune's movement

less sand at edges of dune means that the dune moves forward faster here

Settlement in desert areas occurs mainly where water is available for farming. **Oases** are supplied by underground water, and some rivers which have their source in wetter regions can flow across a desert (for example, the Nile).

Development

Development is a general term which covers standard of living and overall quality of life, as well as general levels of wealth or poverty. Richer countries are described as **more economically developed** (MEDC or the North) and poorer countries as **less economically developed** (LEDC or the South or the Third World). More developed countries (MEDCs) tend to be industrialised, and have good transport, communication, education and health care systems.

The wealth of a country is measured by the value of all the goods and services produced in a year (and takes account of exports and imports). The total figure is called the **Gross National Product** or GNP. This figure is divided by the number of people in the country to give the GNP per person. This is used to compare countries. Other ways of identifying more and less developed countries are also used. They help to give a fuller picture of the differences between countries. Some of these **indicators of development** are life expectancy, population per doctor and infant mortality.

Factors affecting development include: population growth, levels of ill-health and disease, literacy levels, trade, environmental difficulties, quality of transport networks, levels of technology and access to the money needed to finance change.

SEE ALSO Less developed countries (LEDCs), More developed countries (MEDCs), Quality of life

Earthquakes

Earthquakes are shocks on the Earth's surface, resulting from movements of rocks within the crust. The point of movement within the crust is the **focus**. The place on the surface that receives the greatest shock is the **epicentre**. Earthquakes usually take place where the crust's plates are moving against each other (at plate boundaries).

Earthquakes are recorded on a **seismograph** and their intensity is measured on the **Richter Scale**. Earthquakes have **primary effects** (for example, the immediate collapse of a building) and **secondary effects** (for example, fires resulting from broken gas pipes and electricity cables).

Economic activities

Economic activities (jobs that we do) are usually grouped into three **sectors**:
- The **primary sector** includes work in farming, fishing, forestry, mining and quarrying.
- The **secondary sector** includes work in manufacturing industry (making things).
- The **tertiary sector** includes work in services, such as retailing, transport, finance and public services (such as education).

Sometimes an additional **quaternary sector** is identified. This refers to work involving information and ideas, such as research and development or information and communication technology (ICT).

SEE ALSO Farming, Manufacturing industry, Services

Ecosystems

An **ecosystem** is a natural system in which plants and animals are linked to each other and their environment. Examples of large scale ecosystems (**biomes**) are tropical rainforest, savanna and temperate deciduous forest. These ecosystems are affected by geology, soils, climate, relief and the actions of people. Ecosystems also exist on smaller scales, for example, a pond. **Food chains** exist in ecosystems; these start with plants because they make their own food (by photosynthesis), and so they are called **producers**. Animals that obtain their energy by eating plants are called **consumers**. Ecosystems are vulnerable to human interference, so, for example, if a polluting substance affects one part of the system it will also affect others.

Relationships in an ecosystem

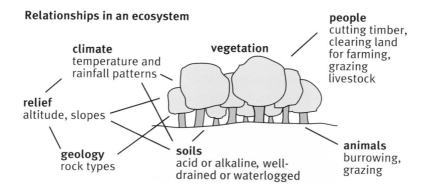

climate
temperature and
rainfall patterns

vegetation

people
cutting timber,
clearing land
for farming,
grazing
livestock

relief
altitude, slopes

geology
rock types

soils
acid or alkaline, well-
drained or waterlogged

animals
burrowing,
grazing

A food chain in a pond, a small-scale ecosystem

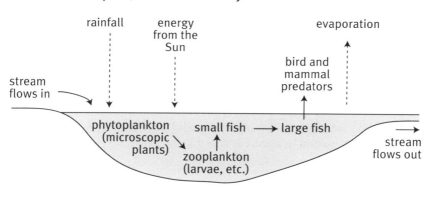

rainfall

energy
from the
Sun

evaporation

bird and
mammal
predators

stream
flows in

phytoplankton
(microscopic
plants)

small fish → large fish

zooplankton
(larvae, etc.)

stream
flows out

SEE ALSO Savanna, Tropical rainforests, Vegetation

Energy

Energy supplies are absolutely vital to modern life. In general, the world is dependent on **fossil fuels**. These are coal, oil and gas, which are fossils because they were all formed from the remains of plants and animals many years ago. The distribution of fossil fuels depends on the underlying geology, and some countries have little or none. The burning of fossil fuels produces carbon dioxide, which is a **greenhouse gas** and plays a major role in **climate change**. Fossil fuels are non-renewable and one day they will run out.

Continued overleaf

Alternative renewable energy supplies are important for two reasons:

- to cut down the greenhouse gases and reduce **global warming**
- to save fossil fuel supplies so they last longer (partly because they have important uses as industrial raw materials).

Alternative renewable energy sources include:

- **Hydro-electric power (HEP)** harnesses the energy of running water (this is widely developed already in many MEDCs).
- **Solar energy** has the potential to heat water directly or to produce electricity (depending on the technology used).
- **Wind energy** is already being produced by wind turbines in MEDCs.
- **Wave and tidal energy** are being developed (although sites for the latter are fairly limited, costs are very high, too).
- **Geothermal energy** is produced from underground water heated by volcanic activity, or by forcing water down under pressure to hot rock deep below the surface. It is turned into steam and used to produce electricity at the surface.
- **Biomass** (generally burning wood) can also be renewable if the trees used for fuel are replaced by new planting, so there is no overall loss to resource supplies. Emissions from burning wood are counteracted by new growth which absorbs carbon dioxide. (This is used a lot in LEDCs.)

Reducing the amount of energy used is an important way of **conserving energy** resources, cutting pollution and reducing global warming. Apart from using alternative energy sources, ways of doing this include:

- developing transport that is more fuel efficient
- increasing public transport use
- insulating buildings to cut heat loss
- constructing buildings that are better insulated to cut heat loss and which make use of the Sun's heat
- cutting the use of air conditioning by designing buildings which keep cool in hot climates and in summer
- designing products so that less energy is used in their manufacture.

SEE ALSO   Renewable and non-renewable resources,
Resource use and the environment

Environmental impact

Human activity has an impact on the environment because all activities cause some kind of change. The challenge is to ensure that any damage is limited. Unfortunately, the effect is often great, causing severe pressures on the local environment. This can include the **natural environment** and the **human environment**. People, as well as plants, animals, soil, the general landscape and the climate can be harmed. The results of such activities cause conflicts.

An example of environmental impact is opencast coal mining. The surface rock is stripped away to get at coal which is near the surface. This is dug out and taken away and the surface rock and soil are replaced and replanted. While the mining is going on there is heavy traffic, noise from blasting and machinery, dust, possible destruction of valuable landscape and damage to people's health.

Often there is strong opposition from local people and others concerned with the environmental impact. This conflicts with the views of the developers of the site. Other local groups, the local council and the national government may be in favour for other reasons, such as the jobs that would be created.

SEE ALSO Environmental issues, Resource use and the environment

Environmental issues

There are concerns about the environment at all scales from the local, through the national, and then to the global scale.

Local scale issues are usually easily recognised and the causes of the problems are usually local, such as the pollution from a copper smelter or the noise from a nearby motorway.

At the national level, environmental problems reflect broader problems, such as shortage of land for housing, limited water supplies or pollution levels generally. At this scale, too, there are the effects of broader problems which may affect particular environments, such as deforestation or soil erosion and problems which cross borders, such as acid rain.

At the global scale, major problems that have an effect worldwide or over large areas of the world are the main concern.

Deforestation is a problem in all forested areas but it is the loss of rainforests that receives most attention. Rainforests are important: for their enormous variety of life or biodiversity; as the source of many plants now cultivated for food and industry; for the 25% of medicines which are based on rainforest products; for protecting lower lands against flooding, as well as reducing soil

Continued overleaf

erosion in higher areas; and because they absorb enormous amounts of carbon dioxide (see 'global warming' below). Rainforests are being destroyed by logging for timber, by clearing land for cultivation and grazing (usually by burning), by the creation of reservoirs, and by opencast mining.

Global warming (or climate change) is the most important of the world scale issues. Carbon dioxide produced by the burning of fossil fuels over the last two hundred years has increased causing the **greenhouse effect**. The overall effect of this is an increase in temperature. This is causing rising sea levels and climate changes, which include higher temperatures, more drought in some areas and more rain in others, and more and stronger hurricanes.

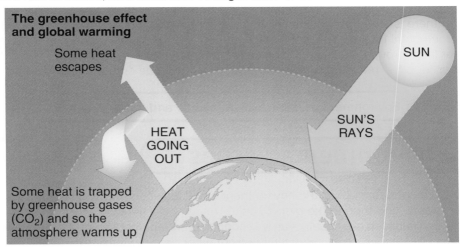

The greenhouse effect and global warming

Some heat escapes

SUN

HEAT GOING OUT

SUN'S RAYS

Some heat is trapped by greenhouse gases (CO_2) and so the atmosphere warms up

SEE ALSO Energy, Environmental impact, Sustainable development

Farming

Subsistence farming is the production of food for the basic needs of the farmer's family. Types of subsistence farming include:

- **shifting cultivation** such as where small areas of forest are cleared and the land is cultivated for a few years until it loses its fertility; then a move is made to a new location
- **intensive subsistence farming** such as the cultivation of rice in south and east Asia

- **nomadic herding**, such as the keeping of cattle in areas of tropical grassland in Africa.

Most subsistence farmers sell some of what they produce because they need cash to pay for items such as tools or health care.

Commercial farming is the production of crops and animal products for sale. Some important types are:

- **Pastoral farming** involves the rearing of animals for meat and products, such as milk and wool. **Extensive** pastoral farming involves grazing animals at a low density on a large area of land, for example, cattle ranching in the western USA. **Intensive** pastoral farming involves large numbers of animals on a small area of land, for example, dairy farming. Much pig and poultry farming is very intensive with animals being reared indoors.

- **Arable farming** is the production of crops. It is usually **capital intensive**, with large sums being spent on machinery, fertilisers and pesticides.

- **Mixed farming** involves a mixture of crops and animals.

- **Plantation farming** is the large-scale production of crops for export in tropical areas. Many plantations are owned by large international companies.

Farming systems are often shown in diagram form to summarise the workings of a type of farming (or just one farm).

Systems diagram of an arable farm, the Fens, East Anglia

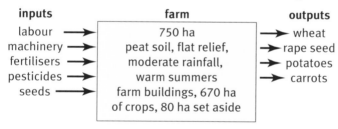

inputs	farm	outputs
labour	750 ha	wheat
machinery	peat soil, flat relief,	rape seed
fertilisers	moderate rainfall,	potatoes
pesticides	warm summers	carrots
seeds	farm buildings, 670 ha of crops, 80 ha set aside	

SEE ALSO Rural areas

Floods

In a flood water flows over land that is not normally under water. Most floods result from rivers overflowing after a period of heavy rainfall. If the ground is already saturated with water, or if rainfall is particularly heavy, there will be much **run off** (or overland flow) into rivers. Floods are natural events, but become a **hazard** when people live in areas likely to flood. Scientists predict that global warming will result in large areas being flooded in the future due to the melting of ice at the Poles. The major effects of floods are loss of life, damage to housing and other buildings, disruption of transport and ruined crops.

Human action can increase the threat of floods, for example, both deforestation and the construction of buildings leads to increased run off into rivers. Measures which can be taken to reduce the hazard of floods include the construction of floodbanks and dams to hold back flood water, and not allowing people to build houses on floodplains.

SEE ALSO Environmental issues, Rivers

Hazards

Hazards are natural events that are a threat to life and property. When they occur on a large scale they are **natural disasters**. Natural hazards include:

- **climatic hazards** hurricanes, tornadoes, drought, floods
- **geological hazards** volcanic eruptions, earthquakes, landslides.

Human activities may increase the threat of many hazards; for example, the felling of forests leads to the more rapid run off of rainwater and makes floods more likely. Long-term environmental problems such as acid rain and global warming are hazards resulting from human activity.

SEE ALSO Environmental issues, Floods, Hurricanes, Landslides

Human features

Much of what we see on the surface of the Earth is the result of human activity. Some of the obvious features are settlements of all kinds, from isolated houses to major cities. However, there are very few areas, especially in more developed countries, which have not been affected in some way by people's actions. Often the changes have been so great that we describe the areas as having human features. The landscape of farming areas is a good example. Fields and their boundary hedges, fences or walls, roads, buildings and patches of woodland have all been created by people. Even moorland in much of upland Britain (which people think of as wild and natural), has been created and maintained by burning and grazing.

The human features in which we are particularly interested in geography include: settlements, urban areas, rural areas, land use patterns, industry and other economic activities, population and the environmental effects of human activity.

Hurricanes

Winds blow in a circular pattern (anti-clockwise in the northern hemisphere) around and into an area of low pressure. **Hurricanes** are areas of intense low pressure, formed over warm tropical seas, which have extremely strong winds. The ocean's heat is the source of energy for a hurricane. Therefore, as a hurricane moves over land it slowly dies down. Damage is caused by high winds, heavy rain, coastal flooding (linked with a **storm surge**, which is caused by a higher sea level created by low pressure) and large waves.

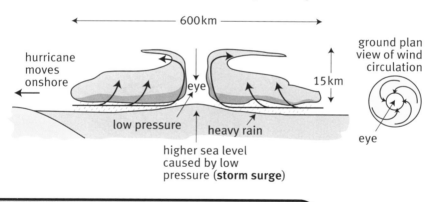

Ice

During the Ice Age, which ended about 25 000 years ago, much of northern Europe was covered by **ice sheets**. They eroded upland areas and deposited **boulder clay** over lowlands. The largest ice sheets existing today are those of Antarctica and Greenland.

Continued overleaf

The higher mountain areas of Britain have glaciated landscapes which are the result of the work of **valley glaciers** during the Ice Age. In major mountain regions such as the Alps, glaciers are still at work. Glaciers erode **U-shaped valleys** and many other distinctive landforms.

The dramatic scenery of glaciated mountain areas has attracted the development of tourism involving both summer and winter visitors. Glacial valleys and lakes provide ideal sites for the development of hydro-electric power stations.

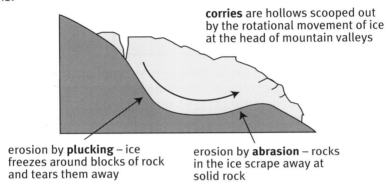

corries are hollows scooped out by the rotational movement of ice at the head of mountain valleys

erosion by **plucking** – ice freezes around blocks of rock and tears them away

erosion by **abrasion** – rocks in the ice scrape away at solid rock

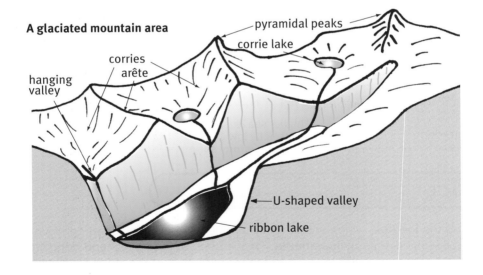

A glaciated mountain area

pyramidal peaks

corrie lake

corries

arête

hanging valley

U-shaped valley

ribbon lake

Interdependence

Interdependence means that something which happens in one place in the world has an effect somewhere else. The term is usually used in relation to countries, but if countries are interdependent, then people and businesses are also interdependent.

- Trade is the simplest illustration of interdependence. Look around your house and you will find products of all kinds from many different countries. These show interdependence because some of the products, such as tropical food products, can only come from other countries, and the countries supplying those products depend on the income from exporting them. However, trade works in other ways, too. When goods are exported from one country to another they may replace a product already made and sold in that country. This may not be good for businesses in that country.
- **Multinational corporations** operate in several countries, and businesses are increasingly using workers in other countries where labour is cheaper, causing **globalisation**.
- Environmental problems can spread between countries. Acid rain is a problem which affects Europe and other industrial areas of the world. Within Europe, air pollution from power stations is blown by the wind and causes the rain that falls to be acid. This happens in countries far from the source of the pollution. The pollution of major rivers, such as the River Rhine, causes problems in other countries downstream from the source of pollution.
- International aid is another example of interdependence. Official aid comes from individual governments or from international agencies such as the United Nations. Non-governmental organisations (NGOs) or development charities such as Oxfam provide small, but important, amounts of aid.
- International tourism has grown enormously in importance. For many small, less developed countries it is a vital part of the economy. Dependence on tourism is risky, however, as a fall in the number of visitors for whatever reason has drastic effects on people's livelihoods.
- Interdependence is often linked to the idea of **global citizenship**. This stresses the fact that we all have a responsibility for the state of the world and a responsibility for other people everywhere. It also means that we must recognise that people around the world do not have equal opportunities. There are huge differences in life chances, justice and quality of life.

SEE ALSO Sustainable development, Tourism, Trade

Landforms

Landforms or physical features reflect the work of rivers, ice and the sea on a wide variety of rock types. Rocks resistant to weathering and erosion will usually form highland areas and those which are less resistant, low-lying plains. Major mountain areas were formed in periods of mountain building, involving the formation of igneous rocks from cooling magma and/or the intense folding of sedimentary rocks.

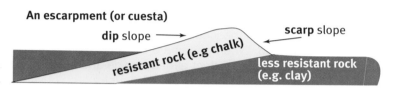

An escarpment (or cuesta)

dip slope ——→   scarp slope ←——

resistant rock (e.g chalk)

less resistant rock (e.g. clay)

A description of the **relief** of an area refers to large-scale landforms such as hills and valleys, plains, plateaus and escarpments.

SEE ALSO Coasts, Deserts, Ice, Rivers, Rock types, Volcanoes

Landslides

A **landslide** is the downhill movement of material. When rock or loose material on a slope becomes **unstable**, a landslide results. A 'trigger' factor or event is needed to cause a landslide – for example, an earthquake; heavy rainfall saturating loose material; or the undercutting of a cliff by rising sea levels.

Landslide of waste material on a hillside

rainfall saturates loose material

loose material becomes unstable and slides down slope

Landslide where a heavy rock type overlies weaker rock

1

sandstone

clay

erosion at base of slope

2

sandstone slides off clay

Latitude and longitude

Latitude and longitude are measures used to describe the exact position of points on the Earth's surface. **Latitude** states the distance of a point north or south of the Equator (latitude 0°) by means of an angular measurement. **Longitude** states the distance of a point east or west of longitude 0° (the Greenwich or Prime Meridian) by means of an angular measurement.

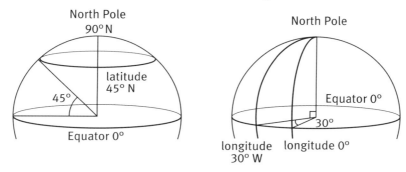

How latitude is calculated   How longitude is calculated

Each degree of latitude and longitude is subdivided into 60 minutes. Thus, the index in an atlas describes the position of New York as 40° 45′ N 74° 0′ W. Lines of latitude are known as **parallels**. All **meridians** of longitude run from the North Pole to the South Pole.

Longitude is used to calculate time at different locations.

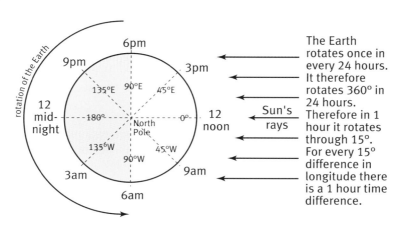

The Earth rotates once in every 24 hours. It therefore rotates 360° in 24 hours. Therefore in 1 hour it rotates through 15°. For every 15° difference in longitude there is a 1 hour time difference.

Less developed countries (LEDCs)

About 80% of the world's people live in the less economically developed countries (LEDCs). They are the poorer countries of the world and are mostly in Africa, Latin America and Asia. They are also known as the Third World or as low income countries. GNP per person is generally below $5000 but there are great differences. Most of the poorest countries are in Africa where Mali, for example, has a GNP per person of only $380 per year.

Population growth rates in LEDCs are generally high. Birth rates are generally high but are falling in most countries. Death rates have fallen considerably. This gives high population growth, even allowing for the deaths from HIV/AIDS in many of the countries in southern Africa.

The majority of the people live in rural areas and work in agriculture, but this pattern is changing rapidly. There has been a great increase in the numbers living in towns and cities, as people leave the countryside to seek a better life elsewhere.

Industrial development varies greatly. Some countries have well established industries and are only included in this group because of the great inequality between citizens. However, the exports of a typical country in this group depend on primary products or raw materials. This is problematic because prices and demand are unreliable, so overseas income is also unreliable. This makes it difficult for these countries to import goods.

SEE ALSO Development, Migration, More developed countries (MEDCs), Quality of life

Manufacturing industry

Manufacturing includes the manufacture of basic goods like steel from original raw materials, assembly products like cars, and high technology products like medicines.

Old industrial areas often developed on coalfields where raw materials (iron ore) and power (coal) were plentiful. Almost all these areas have declined in importance, with competition from other areas. The result has been high unemployment. Regeneration of such areas has been government policy in many countries. Work has been carried out to improve the environment and to attract new industries. New industries have often been given grants and had new buildings provided at low rents to induce them to locate there.

New industrial areas have not been limited to regions with raw materials. They occur in places where communications are good, where there are plenty of well qualified workers, where the environment is pleasant, and in areas where there is a lot of scientific research activity.

Factors of location

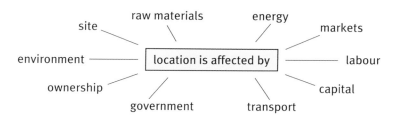

Many countries like LEDCs manufacture goods at cheaper costs than we can. This has led to the decline in manufacturing industry in the UK as firms move to other countries where costs are lower.

SEE ALSO Technology and economic activities

Migration

Migration involves the movement of people from place to place. It can include **permanent migration** when people move to live elsewhere without intending to return. It also includes **seasonal migration** when people move at one time of year and then return, and forced migration by asylum seekers due to persecution. Migration takes place between countries (**international migration**) and within countries (**internal migration**). Within countries there are different kinds of movement:
• from the countryside to towns and cities (in LEDCs)
• from poorer to more prosperous areas, for example, to south-east England
• out of large cities to commute from rural areas (in MEDCs).
Since the expansion of the European Union, there has been large-scale migration from eastern European countries to western Europe for better job prospects. There are many reasons why people migrate. The table groups them together in two sets. Push factors list why people leave a place and pull factors list what attracts them to another.

Continued overleaf

Reasons for migrating

Push factors	Pull factors
poverty	freedom
political persecution	higher living standards
natural disasters	better job prospects
poor job prospects	land
lack of land	health and environment
	education

The proportion of the population living in towns and cities is called the **urbanisation** level. Migration from the countryside to cities is the main type of population movement in LEDCs. It has resulted in huge changes in the population balance between rural and urban areas.

Urbanisation levels (%)

	1960	2006
more developed	60	77
less developed	21	41

More developed countries (MEDCs)

The more economically developed countries (MEDCs) are the **industrialised** countries. They include most of the countries of Europe, North America, Australia and New Zealand as well as Japan and other more recently developed countries of East Asia. They have GNP per person figures averaging $23 690. MEDCs are highly urbanised with up to 90% of the population living in towns and cities. They have well developed manufacturing industries, but most people are employed in service industries. Employment in agriculture varies but is very low compared with less developed countries. Exports are primarily of manufactured goods and most trade in these is between the MEDCs. For example, 60% of the trade of European Union countries is with other member countries.

Overall quality of life is high compared with less economically developed countries (LEDCs) but there are large numbers living in poverty.

SEE ALSO Less developed countries (LEDCs)

Ordnance Survey maps

1:50 000 maps These are known as the Landranger series. 1 cm on the map represents 50 000 cm (or 0.5 km) on the ground. So 2 cm represents 1 km.
1:25 000 maps These are known as the Explorer series. 1 cm on the map represents 25 000 cm (or 0.25 km) on the ground. So 4 cm represents 1 km.
Height on Ordnance Survey maps is shown by **spot heights** (a dot with its height in metres written by it) and **contour lines**. On 1:50 000 maps, the contour interval (the difference in height between adjacent contour lines) is 10 metres. The pattern of contours shows the shape, or **relief**, of the land's surface.
Grid references are used to describe locations on Ordnance Survey maps. The grid lines are spaced at 1 km intervals. Four-figure grid references are used to identify grid squares. Six-figure references are used to describe exact points.

Four- and six-figure grid references

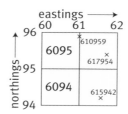

Patterns

Geography is about patterns or the way features are arranged on the Earth's surface. Here are some examples of patterns:

- **Volcanoes and earthquakes** are arranged along the boundaries of the plates of the Earth's crust.
- Highland areas have more **rainfall** than lowland areas.
- **Climatic regions** are arranged in the same way on all the continents. For example, deserts are found on the western sides of continents straddling the Tropics of Cancer and Capricorn.
- **Settlements in mountainous areas** are strung at regular intervals along the valleys.
- **Roads and railways** converge on important settlements.

All of these patterns are best shown on maps. Notice that on a map all these features are shown as dots, lines or patches.

Continued overleaf

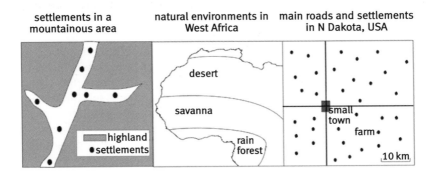

settlements in a mountainous area	natural environments in West Africa	main roads and settlements in N Dakota, USA

■ highland
● settlements

desert

savanna

rain forest

small town

farm

10 km

SEE ALSO Earthquakes, Plate tectonics, Settlement location, Volcanoes

Plate tectonics

Plate tectonics is the study of how the plates which make up the Earth's crust move over time. Earthquakes and volcanic activity occur at or near the boundaries between plates.

- **Destructive (or converging) plate boundary where crust is destroyed**

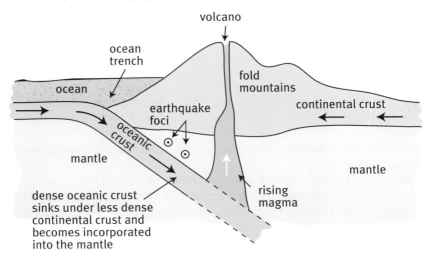

volcano

ocean trench

fold mountains

ocean

earthquake foci

continental crust

oceanic crust

mantle

mantle

dense oceanic crust sinks under less dense continental crust and becomes incorporated into the mantle

rising magma

- **Constructive (or diverging) plate boundary where new crust is created**

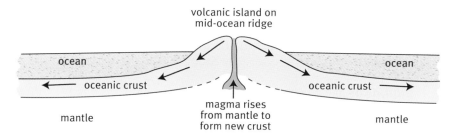

- **Transform (or conservative) plate boundary where plates slide past each other**

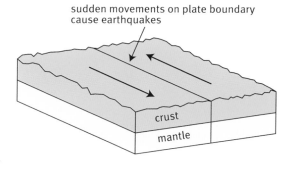

SEE ALSO Earthquakes, Volcanoes

Population and resources

The distribution of population is affected by the distribution of resources. The more crowded areas have more attractive or positive features, and the more empty regions have more hostile or negative features. Within countries the pattern is often related to **climate**, the **relief** of the land and **soil**, but other factors, such as the **location of resources** (important for industrial growth), the location of **major cities** or **historical factors**, can often be just as important.

SEE ALSO Densely populated areas, Migration, Sparsely populated areas

Population growth

The world's population has grown from about 800 million in 1750 to 2500 million in 1950 and is now over 6500 million (6.5 billion). Population growth depends on birth rates and death rates. These are given as the number of births or deaths per thousand people. The difference between them is the **growth rate** or natural increase. This is given as a percentage. The major regions of the world have very different birth, death and growth rates (see table).

Birth, death and growth rates for Africa and Europe

	Birth rate (%)	Death rate (%)	Natural increase (%)
Africa	38	15	2.3
Europe	10	12	−0.2

Movement of people between countries is called **migration** and this also affects the population growth of individual regions and countries.

Factors affecting population size

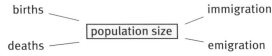

Population change affects countries and regions in many ways. A **decrease** in population causes a shortage of workers and may leave the older part of the population without any support. In agricultural regions there may not be enough people to cultivate the land. An **increase** in population provides a larger workforce, but if there is a shortage of jobs it creates more unemployment. At the same time, in already crowded countries or regions, it creates a shortage of housing, and in agricultural regions a shortage of land.

SEE ALSO Migration

Quality of life

Quality of life used to be described only by comparing levels of wealth using GNP. The term quality of life now includes well-being and the features which make life better, such as life expectancy, levels of education, health, housing

quality, access to clean drinking water and quality of the environment.
In studying the quality of life at any scale, from a single family to a whole
country, it is important to look at a wide range of information.
At the world scale, the United Nations has produced the **Human Development
Index (HDI)**. It compares all the world's countries using measures of health and
education and incomes up to a particular level. If there is a lot of inequality,
meaning that the rich do very well but the poorer majority do badly, it counts
against a country's score. The table shows the top five and bottom five countries
ranked by the HDI. Notice that the top group are all from the more developed
world and the bottom group all from the less developed world.

Human Development Index: top 5 and bottom 5

Top 5	Bottom 5
1 Norway	173 Guinea Bissau
2 Iceland	174 Burkina Faso
3 Australia	175 Mali
4 Ireland	176 Sierra Leone
5 Sweden	177 Niger

SEE ALSO Development

Regions

A region is an area of the world that has **features** which make it different from
other neighbouring areas. For example, a hilly region like the Peak District of
England is different from a lowland region like East Anglia. A region can be
based on any of a number of factors:
1 **relief** (like the example above)
2 **climate** (comparing the climate of the Mediterranean region with the climate
   of north-west Europe)
3 **natural regions** (the tundra of the Arctic regions of North America, Europe
   and Asia, or, in tropical regions, rainforests and savanna or tropical
   grasslands)
4 **economic regions** are based on the main features of the economy (industrial
   regions or agricultural regions, or there may be a city region around a major
   city).

Renewable and non-renewable resources

Renewable resources can be replaced. Forests, for example, can be replanted or, if cutting has been limited, will regenerate by themselves. Water supplies are also renewable. Reservoirs storing water rise and fall according to the season and the amount of rainfall. Water stored in the rocks cannot be replaced as quickly – if water is extracted too quickly, the level of the water table will fall and there may not be enough rainfall to replace it. Water pumped out from deep rocks may take centuries to be replaced.

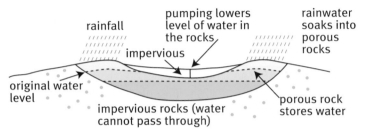

Non-renewable resources cannot be replaced once used. Examples are **fossil fuels** and minerals, like bauxite or iron ore. **Reserves** are deposits of minerals or fossil fuels (such as coal, oil and gas) which are known and which could be exploited under present conditions. Once they have been mined, the reserves available for future use are less. To help conserve non-renewable resources, recycling of the products made from the resources (such as plastics from oil) is possible.

SEE ALSO Energy, Resources, Resource use and the environment

Resources

When we talk about resources we usually mean **natural resources**. These include minerals, rocks, sources of fuel and power, timber, fish, soil, land, water, plants, animals and even scenery. Supplies of resources are known as reserves. The abundance of resources varies. Deposits of metallic minerals that are worth exploiting are mostly concentrated in small areas of the Earth's surface. Some, like bauxite (from which aluminium is made), are fairly common. Others, like gold, are much rarer. Coal is a very common **fossil fuel**. Oil is being used very rapidly so reserves are decreasing. The major source of supply of oil is in the Middle East.

SEE ALSO Environmental issues, Renewable and non-renewable resources

Resource use and the environment

The use of resources has two main sets of effects.
1 Developing and using any resource creates **environmental problems** such as pollution. (This can be seen with mineral extraction.)
2 Land often has **several uses competing for the same space**. (This can be seen almost everywhere but especially in rural areas.)

The effects of mineral extraction and use The diagram shows how the environment can be affected at each stage, from the first land use changes, to the disposal of waste from use of the final product. The unwanted effects can only be prevented by **resource planning and management**. For example, at an opencast coal site the dust problem can be reduced by spraying the area. The noise problem can be reduced by building barriers using the surface rock and soil which has been excavated.

Mineral extraction, use and effects

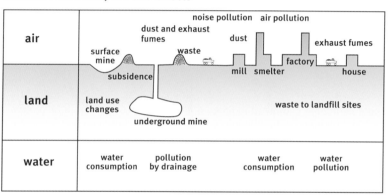

Competing land uses Planning and management are important in areas where there are different land uses all competing with each other. For example, in the Brecon Beacons National Park in Wales the land is used for farming (mainly sheep grazing), forestry, quarrying, water supply reservoirs, military training, recreation and tourism, towns and villages. The area is easily accessible from the coastal areas of South Wales as well as from the West Midlands and the London region, so large numbers of visitors have to be catered for.

SEE ALSO Energy, Human features

Rivers

Rainfall flows into rivers either after flowing across the surface of the land (**run off**) or indirectly through the soil and rocks.

As a river flows downslope much of its energy is used to wear away or **erode** its bed and banks.

- **hydraulic action** is erosion by the direct force of the water itself
- **corrasion** involves the river using the material it is transporting (its **load**) to erode the bed and banks
- **corrosion** (or **solution**) involves the dissolving away of rocks such as limestone
- **attrition** is the reduction in size of pebbles carried by the river, as they collide with each other.

In an upland area, river landforms are mostly the result of erosion. Resistant bands of rock across a river's course may cause **waterfalls**.

Waterfall

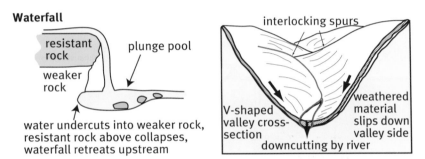

resistant rock

plunge pool

weaker rock

water undercuts into weaker rock, resistant rock above collapses, waterfall retreats upstream

interlocking spurs

V-shaped valley cross-section

weathered material slips down valley side

downcutting by river

The material eroded by a river is transported downstream and as the river's energy decreases, is deposited. In this way, lower down a river's course the river landforms are the result of **deposition**, in addition to erosion.

River landforms in the lower course of a river

oxbow lake

bluffs (steep slopes) on edge of flood plain

meanders

estuary

floodplain

river cliff

deposition on inside of meander

erosion on outside of meander

SEE ALSO Floods

Rock types

Within the Earth's crust there are three main types of rock: **igneous**, **sedimentary** and **metamorphic**.

- **Igneous** rocks are formed from the cooling of molten rock (**magma**), either within the Earth's crust to form rocks with large crystals such as granite or on the surface to form volcanic rocks with small crystals such as basalt.
- **Sedimentary** rocks are formed from small particles, mainly fragments of rock, but also animal shells and plant remains, deposited on the sea bed or, more rarely, on land. As the particles build up they are compressed and cemented together. They occur in distinct layers and many contain fossils. Examples of sedimentary rocks are sandstone, clay, shale, limestone and coal.
- **Metamorphic** rocks have been changed from their original igneous or sedimentary state by great heat and/or pressure. Examples include slate, formed from shale, and marble, formed from limestone.

Igneous rocks and metamorphic rocks are hard and so are resistant to weathering and erosion. Sedimentary rocks are usually softer and so are less resistant. Most metallic minerals are mined from igneous and metamorphic rocks. Useful products of sedimentary rocks include rock salt and coal.

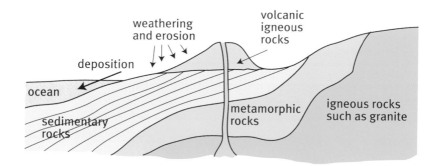

SEE ALSO Plate tectonics

Rural areas

There are a great variety of types of rural areas. For example, intensively-cultivated arable farming areas differ greatly from mountainous areas where sheep graze on the moorlands.

There have been many **changes** in **rural areas** over the last 50 years:

- Farming systems have become more mechanised, and farms have merged to become larger.
- The rural landscape itself has changed, with larger fields as hedgerows have been removed.
- The number of people involved in farming has fallen with mechanisation. Many former farm workers have had to move to towns to work.
- People from towns and cities have moved to the country, converting farm cottages and other farm buildings into larger houses. These people usually either use their village house for weekend visits and holidays, or, if they live there, commute by car to their place of work.
- Many village shops and other services such as schools and bus services have disappeared, as most of the homes have become second homes.

Rural areas are also affected by **urban sprawl**. This affects the land around major cities and even quite small towns. New housing estates, shopping centres, factories and warehouses have covered huge amounts of former countryside as towns and cities have grown.

SEE ALSO Farming, Migration, Services and settlements

Savanna

Tropical grasslands are known as **savanna**. They are found north and south of the Amazon Basin rainforest in South America, over much of Africa between the rainforests and deserts, and in northern Australia. The climate has distinct wet and dry seasons. Trees are present in the savanna besides grasses. There are more trees in wetter areas closer to the rainforest. Towards the desert, there are very few trees in the savanna and even grass becomes sparse. Trees in the savanna are deciduous, shedding their leaves in the dry season, and are adapted to withstand drought. The grazing of wild and domestic animals, together with grassland fires, prevent the savanna developing into forest.

SEE ALSO Ecosystems, Vegetation

Services

Service activities form the **tertiary sector** of the economy. Employment in services can be divided into three main groups:

- **consumer services** such as retailing, catering and tourism
- **public services** such as education, medical services, postal services, banking and the various departments of government
- services which **serve manufacturing and service industries**, including computing and freight transport (some services, such as banking, serve both individual consumers and other companies).

In many MEDCs the service sector is the largest sector of the economy and is growing quickly.

Services and settlements

Settlements in any area are arranged in what is called the settlement **hierarchy**. There is one large settlement, which is the most important, then some smaller ones, and then many smaller ones still.

Hierarchy of settlements

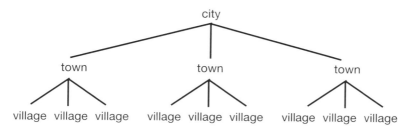

When this hierarchy is shown on a simple map you can see that:

- the large city provides services for the whole area
- the smaller towns each provide services for the areas around them
- the smallest settlements provide services for their immediate area.

Settlement pattern – diagrammatic

Continued overleaf

The reason for this hierarchy of settlements is quite simple. **Services** or goods are not all the same. People are not prepared to travel far for certain goods such as bread – these are called **convenience goods**. Others are more specialist and involve a service or product which people only want occasionally or for which they want to shop around. These are called comparison or **shopping goods**. The bigger, more important places in the hierarchy of shops provide a wide range of different services. The small places only have a limited number of services.

So, we can see that:

- the villages serve a small area with a small range of services
- the market towns serve the area covered by several villages with a much wider range of services
- the city provides the entire area with a very wide range of services including many not available in the other settlements (like the main area hospital).

SEE ALSO Rural areas

Settlement growth

With rural settlements, the reason for growth is often a change in the function of the place. Other activities might begin to develop in what was once just a farming village. The simplest change is when a village attracts people who work in nearby towns and cities so that the place becomes a dormitory settlement. This has also happened to many market towns. The coming of railways and then bus services started this process, but it really took off with growing car ownership. In recent years most small towns in the UK have grown enormously, especially as they have started attracting small-scale industries.

Settlements also decline. For example, many isolated villages in the UK have lost population, and are only occupied by second homeowners in the holiday season.

SEE ALSO Rural areas

Settlement location

Location helps to explain why a settlement developed in a particular place. There are two elements to location: site and situation.

Site is the land on which the settlement was first built. Important points for villages might have been water supply, land for farming, building materials, freedom from flooding, ease of defence or sheltered harbour. Most of these would have been important for towns, too, as would the easy crossing point of a river.

The site of a village

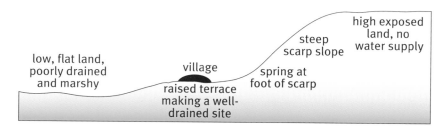

low, flat land, poorly drained and marshy

village

raised terrace making a well-drained site

spring at foot of scarp

steep scarp slope

high exposed land, no water supply

Situation means the position of the settlement within the whole area or region. To be successful, towns must be accessible to the surrounding area. Industrial towns need access to raw materials and to markets. Ports would not be successful without good transport and communications. The map below shows the importance of location for the success of a port.

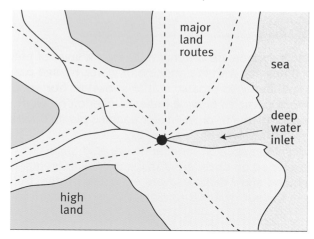

major land routes

sea

deep water inlet

high land

Settlements

Settlements are places where people live. They can consist of permanent buildings or they can be temporary, like the tents of a nomadic group. Permanent settlements range in size from single buildings to megacities. The names used to describe different **types of settlements** vary from country to country. In some, for instance, a place with only a few hundred people might be called a city. The following set of names is generally understood:
- **farmstead** – separate farm or other building
- **hamlet** – small cluster of houses and farms, few or no services
- **village** – larger cluster with a range of services
- **town** – urban settlement, providing a wide range of services for the surrounding area and possibly with some industry
- **city** – large urban settlement, with very wide range of services and industry; it serves a region with a large population including smaller towns as well as villages
- **conurbation** – a large urban area formed by the growth of a major city, swamping surrounding smaller towns.

Rural settlements include farmsteads, hamlets and villages as well as small or market towns. **Urban settlements** include towns, cities and conurbations, so there is some overlap between the two groups.

SEE ALSO Services and settlements, Settlement growth, Settlement location

Soils

Rocks at the Earth's surface are weathered to form a layer of broken material. This material becomes soil with the addition of water, air and organic matter (which includes both decayed organic matter known as **humus** and live organisms). The rock particles provide minerals needed by plants. Humus provides nutrients for plants to grow. Water enables plants to absorb minerals and nutrients.

Soils vary in acidity. Peat soils on moorlands are acid (pH value below 6.0) whereas soils developed on chalk are alkaline (pH value greater than 7.0). Soils also vary in depth and show distinct layers – the **soil profile**. Different mixtures of rock particles in the soil give rise to different soil **textures** such as sandy, clay, silt or loam.

A soil profile

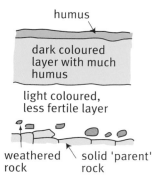

humus

dark coloured
layer with much
humus

light coloured,
less fertile layer

weathered \ solid 'parent'
rock   rock

Soil texture

sandy soil	soil with large particles
clay soil	soil with very fine particles (which stick together)
silt soil	soil with medium-sized particles
loam soil	soil with an even mixture of sand, clay and silt particles

SEE ALSO Ecosystems

Sparsely populated areas

On the world scale, sparsely populated areas are often called empty areas. They include:

- the **hot, arid deserts**
- the **cold** areas, especially in the north of North America and Eurasia
- **mountainous** areas
- many of the **densely forested** areas
- areas generally **lacking resources**
- **isolated** areas.

Within all of these there are small pockets of population, usually where mineral or power resources are being developed, or, in desert areas, where water is available locally. This could be at an oasis where underground water reaches the surface. Alternatively, it could be where a river from a wetter region flows through the area. The River Nile in Egypt is an example of this. The vast majority of Egypt's population live along the river. Elsewhere, people are found at oases. So, we can see that there are sparsely populated areas at the world scale and within individual countries.

SEE ALSO Densely populated areas, Population and resources

Sustainable development

Sustainable development means using the world's resources in such a way that we do not threaten the future of the Earth and the needs of future generations. It involves meeting people's needs, especially the needs of the world's poorest people. It also involves the realisation that the way we make use of the environment can easily destroy it. We must not think that we have the technology and the know-how to put right anything that goes wrong.

The key idea behind sustainable development is that the Earth's natural resources of fish, forests, arable land, water and air are vital to survival. Some of these are renewable but only if they are used properly. When we use those that are non-renewable, of course, they are gone forever. Fair shares is another key idea. People in MEDCs use far more of the Earth's resources than people in LEDCs. They are able to do this by buying resources from LEDCs at low prices. At the small scale there are lots of ways of making improvements and cutting waste and damage to the environment. Recycling is one way. However, on a global scale sustainable development means changes to the way of life of people in MEDCs. We are the ones producing most of the carbon dioxide that causes **global warming**, using paper made from rainforest trees, and using up the world's resources generally.

SEE ALSO Development, Energy, Environmental issues, Interdependence, Renewable and non-renewable resources

Technology and economic activities

New technology has a great effect on economic activity:

- **Older industries** face change when new technology makes their production methods uncompetitive. For example, a steel works with 20 000 workers may be able to produce more with a work force of only 3000. Automation of assembly plants had a similar effect in the car industry.
- **Information technology** has spread the impact of new technologies across service activities, too. The number of people needed for many jobs has fallen, but at the same time new jobs have been created. The Internet provides services that previously were carried out by post or by face-to-face contact and resulted in the globalisation of many industries. Work previously done in the UK can now be carried out in an LEDC for lower wages.

- New technologies have created **new industries** and new industrial areas. For example, Silicon Valley in California, and the Cambridge Science Park in the UK.

SEE ALSO Manufacturing industry, Trade

Tourism

Tourism is a fast growing industry. Most tourists are from MEDCs where people have more money and time for holidays. The development of cheaper air travel has led to the expansion of tourism in LEDCs. For tourism to develop there must be the right attractions or **resources for tourism**. They include:
- climatic advantages such as sunny weather
- coasts with sandy beaches
- landscapes that have attractive scenery or make special activities (such as skiing) possible
- places that have a history and culture which attract tourists
- purpose-built attractions (such as Disney World in Florida).

The advantages of tourism include the influx of money to tourist areas and the creation of jobs. However, there are also problems, for example, employment is often seasonal and tourist developments may damage the environment.

Trade

Trade concerns the movement of goods from the places where they are produced to where they are used. This can be within a country or between countries, when it is referred to as **international trade**. Trade is very important in the economic lives of countries, and the businesses involved employ large numbers of people. Trade belongs to the **tertiary** group of economic activities. Trade has developed because raw materials and manufacturing industry are not distributed evenly around the world. Trade involves **exports** and **imports**. Imports are goods coming from overseas; exports are goods that are sent to other countries.

Continued overleaf

Movements of exports and imports are not always direct. In many instances goods are transported to one place and then sent on to other places. This is known as **entrepôt** trade. Singapore is a good example, as it is at the hub of many shipping routes.

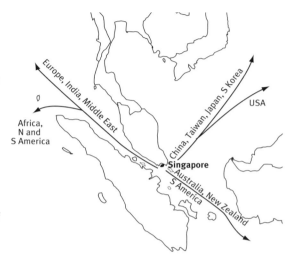

Trade is uneven. Most international trade is between the small number of MEDCs. Most of their exports are manufactured goods. LEDCs send well over half of their exports to MEDCs. About half of LEDC exports are of raw materials or primary products. Many of these countries depend on one or two primary products for almost all their exports.

Relying on **primary product exports** causes problems for LEDCs:

- A fall in demand can mean an almost total loss of export income.
- Prices vary with demand, so if demand goes down so does the price; primary product prices vary much more than prices of manufactured goods, so income is unreliable.
- Prices of manufactured goods increase over time more than those of primary products. This means that countries have to try to export more to pay for the same amount of imports.

Globalisation is tied in with trade. The term describes the way that places are becoming more and more interdependent. This is partly due to the way in which trade in goods and services is changing. International trade is increasing as companies try to find cheaper and cheaper places to make their products. This makes for a greater level of interdependence, but is one-sided in that MEDCs get cheap manufactured goods while the LEDCs making them get little income and unreliable jobs. The increasing use of the Internet has encouraged globalisation.

SEE ALSO Interdependence, Technology and economic activities

Tropical rainforests

Tropical rainforests occur in **equatorial climates**. Temperatures and rainfall totals are high throughout the year. The trees form three distinct layers, the highest layer rising to about 45 metres. There is an enormous variety of species of plants which in turn provide habitats for a rich variety of animal life. The largest areas of tropical rainforest are found in the Amazon Basin of South America, the Congo Basin of Africa and equatorial areas of south-east Asia.

The world's rainforests are under threat from logging and the expansion of farming. The loss of rainforests is a major problem because it means the destruction of animal habitats. Also, run off from the heavy rainfall becomes greater, causing problems of soil erosion and flooding. In addition, the forests act as a major 'lung' for the planet, absorbing carbon dioxide and producing oxygen – we need them to help us with the problem of global warming.

SEE ALSO Ecosystems, Environmental issues, Vegetation

Urban change

Urban change is a world-wide feature. In MEDCs there have been shifts of population within cities and out of big cities. The diagram sums this up (although there has been a movement back to inner city life recently due to redevelopment).

Urban population change in MEDCs

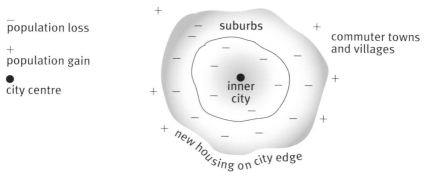

− population loss

+ population gain

● city centre

suburbs

commuter towns and villages

inner city

new housing on city edge

In many MEDCs, **urban spread** has engulfed the countryside as new industrial estates, shopping areas, sports facilities and new housing have been built, all of which require new roads.

Continued overleaf

In LEDCs urbanisation has increased as people have migrated from the countryside to the cities. Even when the total population of a country has increased greatly, the cities have grown at a faster rate due to this **internal migration.**

SEE ALSO Less developed countries (LEDCs), Migration, Rural areas, Urban land uses

Urban land uses

Urban land use maps show what urban areas or parts of urban areas are like at a particular time. So that we can make comparisons over time and between different places, a common system (or classification) is needed. A land use classification identifies:

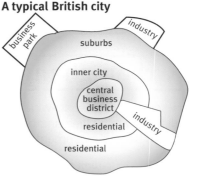

A typical British city

- shops
- offices
- housing
- industry
- open space
- transport.

Comparisons over time show changes. The inner parts of British cities provide an example. They were a mix of densely-packed housing and industry in the early part of the last century. **Redevelopment** from the 1950s onwards led to much industrial land being abandoned. In more recent times, further changes have seen reclamation of industrial land for a variety of uses.

Patterns and models

Urban land use shows patterns that are repeated in one town and city after another. However, there are always differences between places. This is why geographers have produced **models** which are simplified but which highlight the common features. For example, the above diagram of a typical British city shows the city centre or central business district in the middle of the city. The other zones around it are also normal features. If you look at particular cities you will find variations, but the overall pattern will have the features shown in the diagram above.

Cities in different parts of the world vary, so the models are also different. In LEDCs there are different patterns. The diagram below shows just one typical arrangement. The feature that is common to many cities in less developed countries is the existence of squatter areas or **shanty towns** which house many of the poor migrants from the countryside.

A city in a less developed country

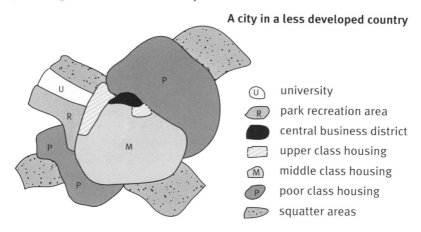

U	university
R	park recreation area
⬛	central business district
▨	upper class housing
M	middle class housing
P	poor class housing
⬭	squatter areas

SEE ALSO Urban change

Vegetation

Vegetation develops in a number of stages over time from a bare surface. The different stages lead to a natural vegetation that exists in a state of balance with the climate of an area. On a world scale, climate is the major factor in determining large groups of plants (**biomes**) such as tropical rainforests. In north-west Europe, for example, where rain falls throughout the year but temperatures vary considerably with the seasons, the natural vegetation is temperate deciduous woodland; the trees' loss of leaves in winter reflects that season's low temperature. Vegetation is often altered by human interference (for example, grazing by cattle or burning) and many forest biomes are threatened by **deforestation**.

SEE ALSO Ecosystems, Savanna, Tropical rainforests

Volcanoes

Most volcanoes are found close to plate boundaries in the Earth's crust. Volcanic eruptions occur when molten rock (**magma**) reaches the Earth's surface. Eruptions can be explosive or continuous. Volcanoes produce **lava**, **ash** and **gases**. Rapid melting of ice and snow on a volcano causes **mud flows**. Although volcanoes are a major hazard to people, volcanic material usually gives rise to fertile soils which attract settlement.

Features of a volcano

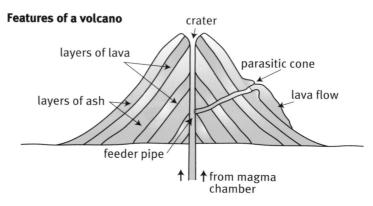

SEE ALSO Plate tectonics, Rock types

Water cycle

The **water** (or **hydrological**) **cycle** is the circulation of water through the atmosphere, oceans and land.

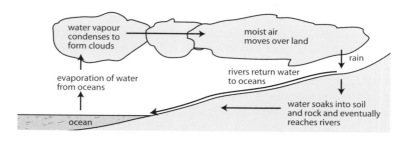

SEE ALSO Rivers

Weathering

Weathering is the breakdown or decomposition of rocks due to the effects of various physical, chemical and biological processes. The main type of **physical weathering** is **freeze-thaw action**, also known as frost shattering.

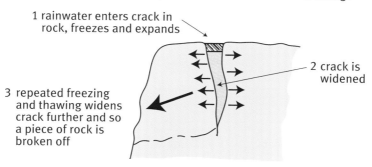

1 rainwater enters crack in rock, freezes and expands

2 crack is widened

3 repeated freezing and thawing widens crack further and so a piece of rock is broken off

Chemical weathering is the result of chemicals in rainwater combining with chemicals in rock minerals, so causing the minerals to change and the rocks to break down. For example, rainwater is a weak carbonic acid which attacks and dissolves away limestone (limestone is calcium carbonate). Chemical weathering is more rapid in warmer and wetter conditions. Polluted air also accelerates chemical weathering.

Biological weathering involves the action of plant roots and burrowing animals; for example, growing plant roots penetrating and widening cracks in rocks. Weathering does *not* involve the removal of rocks. **Erosion** involves the wearing away and removal of rocks by rivers, ice, the wind or the sea. Rock weakened by weathering will be easy to erode.

SEE ALSO Coasts, Ice, Rivers

World map

Test yourself: identify the major countries (1–15), cities (A–K), rivers (r1–r4) and mountain ranges (m1–m3). See page 46 for answers.

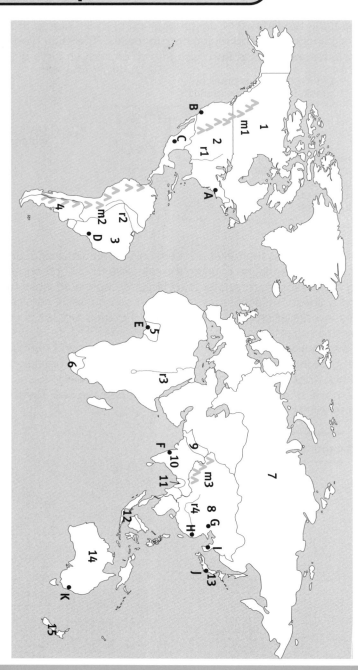

Europe map

Test yourself: identify the major countries (1–20), cities (A–R), seas (1–4) and rivers (rX– rY). See page 46 for answers.

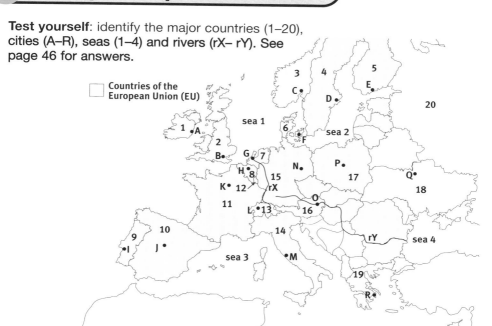

Countries of the European Union (EU)

sea 1
sea 2
sea 3
sea 4

1 A
2
3
4
5
6
7
8
9
10
11
12
13
14
15
16
17
18
19
20

B
C
D
E
F
G
H
K
L
M
N
O
P
Q
R

rX
rY

United Kingdom map

Test yourself: identify the major cities (A–P), mountain areas (1–6) and rivers (rX–rZ). See page 46 for answers.

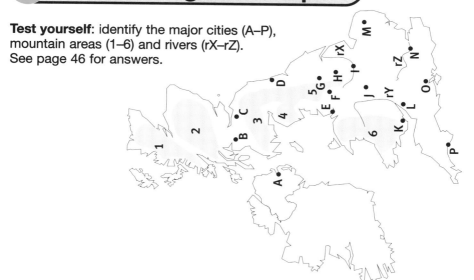

Answers to maps

World map

Countries
1 Canada
2 USA
3 Brazil
4 Argentina
5 Nigeria
6 South Africa
7 Russia
8 China
9 Pakistan
10 India
11 Bangladesh
12 Indonesia
13 Japan
14 Australia
15 New Zealand

Cities
A New York
B Los Angeles
C Mexico City
D Sao Paulo
E Lagos
F Mumbai (Bombay)
G Beijing
H Shanghai
I Seoul
J Tokyo
K Sydney

Rivers
r1 Mississippi
r2 Amazon
r3 Nile
r4 Yangtze

Mountain ranges
m1 Rocky Mountains
m2 Andes
m3 Himalayas

Europe map

Countries
1 Republic of Ireland
2 United Kingdom
3 Norway
4 Sweden
5 Finland
6 Denmark
7 Netherlands
8 Belgium
9 Portugal
10 Spain
11 France
12 Luxembourg
13 Switzerland
14 Italy
15 Germany
16 Austria
17 Poland
18 Ukraine
19 Greece
20 Russia

Cities
A Dublin
B London
C Oslo
D Stockholm
E Helsinki
F Copenhagen
G Amsterdam
H Brussels
I Lisbon
J Madrid
K Paris
L Bern
M Rome
N Berlin
O Vienna
P Warsaw
Q Kiev
R Athens

Rivers
rX Rhine
rY Danube

Seas
1 North Sea
2 Baltic Sea
3 Mediterranean Sea
4 Black Sea

United Kingdom map

Cities
A Belfast
B Glasgow
C Edinburgh
D Newcastle
E Liverpool
F Manchester
G Leeds
H Sheffield
I Nottingham
J Birmingham
K Cardiff
L Bristol
M Norwich
N London
O Southampton
P Plymouth

Rivers
X Trent
Y Severn
Z Thames

Mountain areas
1 North-West Highlands
2 Grampian Mountains
3 Southern Uplands
4 Lake District
5 Pennines
6 Cambrian Mountains